Rufus

Rufus
The Tale of a Dog

by

David McCune

authorHOUSE®

AuthorHouse™
1663 Liberty Drive
Bloomington, IN 47403
www.authorhouse.com
Phone: 1-800-839-8640

First published by AuthorHouse   01/17/2012

ISBN: 978-1-4685-4543-2 (sc)
ISBN: 978-1-4685-4542-5 (hc)
ISBN: 978-1-4685-4541-8 (ebk)

Library of Congress Control Number: 2012901082

Printed in the United States of America

Rufus

Introduction

At least once a day I'm asked, "So what's it like living in downtown?" My response has been the same since I moved to the end townhouse at 300 Hay two years ago. "This is the only place I considered to live when I moved back from the beach," I say with enthusiasm.

I enjoyed living on the island of Ocean Isle Beach, North Carolina, for fourteen years prior to moving back to Fayetteville, North Carolina. Looking out at the ocean and watching the boats and ships travel the Intercoastal Waterway evoked a sense of constant movement.

In downtown Fayetteville, the intrigue and excitement of living here is also constant movement. Hay Street, like the living body of the ocean with tides and waves, changes from hour to hour. And, the train tracks are like the swift waters of the Intercoastal Waterway. Sure, the train's whistles can be a little unnerving at times, but the ambiance and mystique of adventure as the wheels spin turn the sounds to a faint whisper.

The day always begins with Rufus, my Red Irish Terrier, and me walking to Festival Park. Depending on Rufus' waking hour, this sets the day into motion. "OK, little buddy, let me get your leash on your collar so we can head out this morning," I say as the leash snaps.

The front door closes and the cold air briskly strikes my face. I look down at Rufus as the wind rustles his red, wiry coat. "Come on, Rufus, let's go ahead and get the show on the road," I say, with a gentle tug to his red, retractable leash.

WHEN WILL MASTER quit pulling at me . . . I need to sniff and see just what's been around the front door, sniff . . . sniff . . . sniff. He often forgets who is in charge of security at the fort. It is me, Rufus! Need to get this out at least once in a while! Now, going down to the walkway to nowhere and the big empty building beside the big grassed area. Must be one of those political jobs they talk about on 640AM. Love that channel, especially when Shawn Hannity comes on . . . makes me proud to be an American dog. Might just call in some day and give a dog's perspective.

Yep, there's the airplane that got caught in the wires. Been there since I was a pup. Would think that someone would have taken it down by now. Human government is so slow. Now, if dogs were in charge, we wouldn't have gotten it stuck up there in the first place.

I have thought and come to the conclusion that what holds us dogs back are our paws, can't do a lot with paws. But we have tails. And we can wag our tails twenty-five different ways to communicate. I saw a poor dog the other day that lost his tail. All he had was a little nub and attempted to wag. I couldn't understand a word he said. It sort of reminded me of master's new Paris Hilton bobble head doll. I don't know what I'm going to do with him at times!

Chapter One

A lonely, cold, Red Irish Terrier roams the isolated streets. Abandoned, he searches for food and security. An old cardboard box and a few morsels of food are his staples as he takes on the role of a street dog.

Drawn from instinct and in search of companionship, the scruffy little dog leaves the security of his makeshift home. Fast moving and noisy cars, trucks, and buses keep him on guard as he ventures out on his quest to discover his destiny. Three blocks away in a three-story townhouse, a lonely human soul patiently waits and the little dog is drawn toward his emptiness. A scratch at the door and a few travailing whimpers alert the resident of a visitor, and their connection is made.

"Hey, little fellow . . . where did you come from?" I smile as I lift the little dog and nestle him securely to my warm chest. "You look sort of scared and lonely. Would you care to come in for a little treat?" I ask. The dog's eyes open wide, and his head sinks softly onto my shoulder.

I gently close the door and proceed to the elevator. "I bet you've never been on one of these," I say, pushing the button to call the elevator to the first floor. The door opens, and the new noise and vibrations startle the dog. "I need to close the door and we're going to go for a little ride," I say comfortingly and slowly close the sliding door to the elevator. Having never experienced controlled vertical movement, the dog digs his nails into me during the short ride. The elevator stops and I place him on the soft carpeted elevator floor and then open the door. He quickly exits the elevator and runs to the warmth and smell of the kitchen.

"Hey, little buddy, would you like some warm milk and a little bread?" I eagerly ask. His tail, then his entire body begins wagging. This is one hungry puppy. Completely devouring the bowl of food in minutes, he ventures into the living room. Sniffing and scurrying, he finds a chair and a safe place to rest his legs. Moments later the curly red-haired puppy is sound asleep. A few hours later, with a slight yawn and a little twitch, the pup awakes to a safe, secure new world.

The little guy must be lost and his owners are frantically searching for him, I began to think. "A quick trip to the animal shelter will be the best bet to find your owners and see if you have a microchip under your coat," I say, gently picking him up.

Riding in my car to the animal shelter, the young pup sleeps soundly in the seat beside me. "We're here, little buddy, let's see if these good people inside can tell me anything about you," I say as I lift him up and out of the car. Not having a collar or leash, I hold him to my chest and walk toward the animal shelter. As the sliding doors open, I begin to feel concerned about the future of my new-found little friend.

"Hello, Happy People, how is everyone today?" I greet the employees in the reception area.

"What can we do for you, Sir?" the receptionist pleasantly asks.

"I found this little dog in downtown Fayetteville and need to report him missing," I reply. The pup watches the dialogue between the two and his head moves cautiously left and right.

"First, let's see if he has a computer chip implant under his coat," she says while examining him with the detection equipment. "No chip on him," she says sternly.

"My, so now what do we do?"

"We need to fill out a report and take his picture to post on our bulletin board," she replies while pointing at the bulletin board across from her.

"So what can you tell me about the dog?" I ask.

"Well, let's see, he looks like he's around five or six months old . . . and he has carpet paws," she replies, smiling.

"Carpet paws? What are carpet paws?" I ask, laughing just a little.

"That means he has lived inside and has not spent a lot of time on the street," she laughs.

"Thanks for everything, if you hear anything just give me a call," I say, lifting the pup.

"Have a nice day and thanks for bringing him in."

Back in the car the little dog quickly falls to sleep again on the passenger seat. "Well, little guy . . . I guess you're my responsibility for now," I say as I gently pat him on the head.

HAVING DECIDED TO go into work with my new little friend, I pull into my parking place in front of our business. McCune Technology/Fayetteville Steel is a complete metal fabrication facility and metals warehouse. Simply put, we make things out of metal.

"Hey, little guy, let's go in so you can meet some new people," I say, bouncing him up and down in my arms as I walk into the reception area.

"What's your name, boy?" Louise asks. The little pup looks at her and licks her hand. I place the pup on the floor and he stands up on his hind legs, walks around, then lies down.

"Remember *Star Wars?* Remember Chewbacca? He sort of looks like him when he walks around and is the same color of the alien. I could call him Chewy for short . . . maybe that will be a good name for him," I say, laughing. Not getting a positive response, the name Chewbacca is definitely out.

During the past year I played the part of young Rufus Edmisten, North Carolina Attorney General, in a TV series. "I like the name Rufus . . . you look like a Rufus. What do you think of the name Rufus?" I ask the little dog. Not hearing a reply, "Rufus is your name unless someone claims you," I say, patting him on his head and then scratching under his long-haired chin.

"Come on, Rufus, let's go outside," I call, opening the door for him. Rufus follows me out to the side of the building and quickly runs round and round in large circles. Suddenly, he lifts his torso and flies up through the air . . . a little longer than a normal dog should be able to jump.

"Rufus, that was a trick I have never seen before," I say, commenting on his spectacular feat. Following me back into the building, Rufus remains close by my side.

Chapter Two

Kenny O'Brian is my first memory of a dog. The Irish Setter was my five-year-old brother Bob's dog. Kenny would knock me down and, I was told, pooped in the basement. Only Bob appeared to like the dog. Late one evening strangers came into our home on Burke Street in Parkersburg, West Virginia. The strangers quickly left with Bob's dog and he was in tears.

Next, Spot came into our lives when I was in second grade. She was a Heinz 57 mix and had a large black patch on her side. Spot seemed to be the only logical name. She lived with the family for over fifteen years. She was a good dog.

Then came Z. With an idea and a $35 investment, I founded McCune Technology in 1975. I was one of the original inventors of the rear window louver seen on hatchback cars of the seventies. I had a Datsun 240Z, so the name Z was a natural fit for the little black dog that entered and exited my life years ago. He just left one day never to return.

Between 1974 and 1975, Malcolm Bricklin introduced the Bricklin automobile. This futuristic car had a pretty much indestructible body and gull wing doors. Being a fastback, this car was the perfect candidate for my rear window louver. The Grafinger's, Harry and Susan, owned a Bricklin and ran an exotic pet store in Fayetteville. I would work on their Bricklin and in trade for a set of louvers, I ended up with a dingo.

A dingo is the wild dog from Australia that roams in packs and breeds for life. When the mate dies, their life partner lies down beside them and starves to death. An unusual dog needed an unusual name.

Nina was determined. Nina could be violent. Though a member of the canine family, Nina did not have a typical dog brain. If chasing something, she would not stop under the tree and bark . . . she would climb the tree as fast as a cat. Some desired to prove that Nina would accept them. She accepted or snapped. Some were slow, and she left a mark.

On her plus side, Nina was dedicated to the family . . . our family became her surrogate mate. She lived fourteen years.

In 1994, I became the statistic of a divorce and was living at McCune Technology. One day a dog showed up at the building and scratched at the door. I let him in. The dog walked into my office and eased himself into one of the club chairs. Having him there gave me a sense of comfort and helped during times of loneliness.

During a prescribed visitation, my children, David Jr. and Sarah, were spending the evening at McCune Technology. Being within compliance, I had to return them to their court-assigned residence. The mystery dog had only been with me for two days, so I left him outside during their return procedure.

Sometime after we left, he either chased us or he ran up by the main road in front of the building. Upon my return I found him on a bloodstained pavement. I pulled his motionless body off the road and buried him. Loss of the future can be just as disturbing as the absence of the past.

Chapter Three

"Come on, Rufus, let's go back to my office," I say, patting my leg. He follows close by as we go through the doors.

My office consists of a large lab, two joined personal rooms, a small kitchen with seating, and a bathroom. Artwork covers the walls. Electronic, painting, and mechanical equipment are on the counters, tables or in the shelves and drawers. An elaborate drum set, synthesizer, electric bass guitar, amplifying and recording equipment dominate my personal space. A little dog can get into big trouble here. Looking up, Rufus gazes around the rooms. He begins sniffing and finds his way to the drum set.

"Hey, Rufus, do you want to hear some new noises?" I call out from the drum throne. A few hits on the bass drum and the high hat immediately grab his attention. He appears to enjoy the new sound. I continue as he curls up under the largest floor tom-tom.

When I was a teenager, I decided to buy a set of drums. After putting them together and then admiring my purchase, I began teaching myself how to play. Years passed and the desire to play ceased. I secretly wanted to buy a new set of drums, but never followed through on my adult dream.

At the age of 51, I decided to learn how to dance. Sure, I had danced before . . . like the time I attempted this body movement after a seventhgrade sock hop in the confines of my locked bedroom with my radio playing. After that experience my performing abilities never blossomed. Now, as middle-aged adult, I was going to do something that I feared and something completely out of the box: I began taking professional dance lessons twice a week with my instructor, Sunday.

In the end, I competed in a dance event and shocked my family. With rhythm in my blood and a song in my heart, I was now ready to buy a set of drums. And I did.

Waking up from his much-needed nap, Rufus is ready to explore the world and relieve his bladder. Again, Rufus starts to run around in circles and jumps into the air. He appears to float in the air as time stands still. I'm tempted to have someone else observe this phenomenon of nature, then I decide to wait

Chapter Four

Our family summer vacation is here and Rufus, now part of the family, is invited to the mountains of North Carolina. After a five-hour trip, we meet everyone there.

Louie is the Weimaraner that belongs to my daughter and son-in-law. He is like a big awkward kid with a heart of gold. Rufus loves Louie. Rufus' colorful red tail constantly wags when Louie is around. Sarah is my daughter, so Rufus is Louie's uncle, in dog relationships. Rufus weighs around 20 pounds, and Louie is under 100 lbs and still filling out. Rufus and Louie enjoy each other's company.

Bark, bark . . . growl. Bark, bark, ruff, ruff . . . snarl, ruff, bark . . . bark. "Hey Rufus, have you ever seen so many sticks?" Louie asks, looking up at all of the tall trees surrounding them.

"Where do you think all of these sticks come from, Louie . . . do you think they fall from the sky?" Rufus asks, also looking up.

"Of course they fall from the sky, Rufus . . . they sure don't grow up from the ground," Louie snaps back.

"This is what I call a stick smorgasbord," responds Rufus, chewing on a choice stick.

BEING A RED Irish Terrier, Rufus is seldom separated from his leash while visiting the outside world. His breed forgets the past and focuses on the future as they chase anything that moves.

While engaged in this frenzy of motion, Rufus completely forgets his name and the person who pleads while calling out, "Rufus . . . Rufus . . . come here, boy." Whatever has moved has captured his attention. The movement is within eyesight and the chase of his prey outweighs everything.

Months ago his victim was a mounted police horse. I am not sure who was shocked the most, the officer or his horse. Eventually Rufus gave up on the fearless attack and retreated.

THE MOUNTAIN HOUSE sits on the top of its own hill. This creates some form of invisible protective fence. Hesitant, I release Rufus from his leash and he runs happily with his buddy Louie. Quickly, he becomes aware the constraint of the leash no longer tugs his neck. He is free.

"Come here, Rufus . . . come here, boy," I sternly call him. Without hesitation, he turns and runs toward me. "Now that is a good buddy. Good boy, Rufus," I say reassuringly as he licks my hand. "OK, have a good time playing with Louie." I send him off, feeling safer about my little buddy and the surroundings.

"Look, Daddy, there are blackberries over here," Sarah calls out, holding up a large, juicy berry for our inspection. Rufus quickly turns toward Sarah and investigates her discovery. In no time, Rufus is up on his hind legs walking around the bush and having his fill of the sweet blackberries. I do believe Rufus could live off the land finding all sorts of delectable treats.

Rufus and Louie begin to venture out. Before long they make a pronounced path down the hill. As sticks are thrown, both dogs race up and down in the exciting game of fetch. Though trampled more than once, Rufus never backs down to Louie.

Sarah decides join in the fun and run down the newly-formed path. With just a little caution, she releases her body to the over forty-five degree descent. Ten feet into her journey, Sarah loses her footing and slips. Down she goes ever so quickly until she finds something to grab on to and stop the fall. Louie and Rufus run to her rescue. Sarah tightly grasps Louie's collar and he helps pull her up the hill to safety. Sarah is scraped up a little and sore. Unfortunately, two weeks later would reveal she landed in poison ivy.

"Peanut Party . . . . Peanut Party!" I call out, throwing a small handful of nuts into the air. Rufus and Louie quickly swarm the area to find the fun little morsels.

"Don't feed Louie peanuts," Sarah says, somewhat scolding.

"Sarah, a few peanuts aren't going to hurt Louie . . . and, besides, he's on vacation. He needs to live a little."

"Dogs need to eat dog food, and that's all there is to it!"

The Peanut Parties will continue when Sarah isn't around. I'm sure George Washington Carver would not have objected.

The week comes to an end and Rufus and Louie say their goodbyes. Vacations are just as fun for dogs as humans.

Chapter Five

I recently read that an average dog can successfully recognize up to one hundred words and their IQ is that of a two-year-old. Lately, I have been talking more to Rufus, attempting to build his listening cognitive vocabulary skills. Besides his name, one of Rufus' favorite words is Grandpa.

Rufus enjoys riding in the car. Usually on the weekends, we leave downtown Fayetteville and head to Sunset Beach, North Carolina. Five miles from my father's house we cross over highway 17, which intersects a McDonald's restaurant. Rufus sits up and begins looking around.

"Hey, Rufus, we are almost at Grandpa's house . . . you're getting ready to see Grandpa!" I announce. The closer we approach Dad's neighborhood, the more excited Rufus becomes. When we pull in the driveway, Rufus goes into a frenzy. He is ready to escape from the car and see his loving Grandpa.

Dad's front door opens and Rufus runs into the house in search of his Grandpa. Once found, the two are equally excited to see each other. When they both calm down, Dad retreats to his leather sofa to watch television and Rufus searches the house for his stuffed rabbit.

"Rufus . . . Rufus, where is your baby . . . can you find your baby?" I coax him. In no time flat he finds the rabbit and happily runs through the house with it held firmly in his closed mouth.

Rufus is a lot of companionship for Dad. Mom lives in an assisted living facility in Fayetteville. For the past ten years she has suffered from Alzheimer's. Two years ago, Dad was no longer able to take care of Mom and we sadly moved her to Fayetteville. Prior to the move, Mom would sit in this sun room and watch the golfers swing their clubs.

Now, Rufus watches the golfers swing their clubs. Toward the end of her stay at Sunset Beach, Mom's enjoyment came from her simple pleasure of sitting in the sun room. Now, Rufus periodically takes her place on the couch and helps fill some voids of absence by acting as an unexpected surrogate.

MATT, MY SON-IN-LAW, and Sarah taught Louie to relieve himself outside by calling to him, "Go potty, Louie. Go potty." I just could not get myself to use this phrase while training Rufus. Instead, while he's in the act, I say, "Good buddy, Rufus . . . you're part of the good buddy system . . . everyone likes a good buddy."

Now when we walk and he's taking just a little too much time, and especially if it's raining, I call out, "Let's be a good buddy, Rufus." This word skill he learned is effective, as he quickly eliminates on a cold and wet day.

Chapter Six

Staying at McCune Technology is not fun, at times, for Rufus. The windows are up high and the only time he is outside is to relieve himself. People frequent my office and he happily greets them. I am constantly coming and going from the office and this unsettles him. He appears to lack purpose and recognizes this feeling of inadequacy. Helping to boost his sense of worth and self esteem, I have been leaving him at home to guard the fortress.

In Ireland the Red Irish Terrier has a highly defined role. This small dog (Rufus is not aware that he is small and everyone is keeping this secret from him.) is bred to be a hunter and guard dog.

They are also known to be the protectors of the Wee People. From my research, it is not well defined if the "Wee People" are small Irish citizens or leprechauns. Regardless, the terriers are excellent guard dogs. At the slightest sound, Rufus races into action to find the mildest disturbance. He listens, then sounds his barking alarm to ward off the enemy. The barks and growls that come forth sound fierce and are rather shocking coming from this somewhat little dog.

I'm sure while alone in the house Rufus monitors the residence equal to the best security system available. Each of the three floors has low windows and doors, so he can easily see any trouble. Yes, Rufus the hunter is on guard . . . violators watch out.

EARLY, SOMETIMES JUST a little too early, Rufus is ready to begin the day. Often before the sun rises, Rufus likes to go out. No matter where we are he has his choice places to go. Usually the location is close to a half mile away. When ready, the Good Buddy does his business, then we return home to make fresh coffee, a welcome reward for me.

We left early one morning in downtown Fayetteville and headed in the usual direction of Festival Park. Arriving at the large open area of Festival Park, we were greeted by three large, skinny, barking street dogs. Rufus immediately stood up tall on his hind legs, raised his paws, and barked loudly. The three street dogs fled with their tails between their legs. This is an old trick that Eskimos use when they accidentally run into a large predatory animal. I guess it must work.

Chapter Seven

Often, I visit my mother in the assisted living facility. She, along with twenty-three other people, is confined to the third floor where the residents are grouped into three categories: old age, dementia, and Alzheimer's. Asking prior permission, I take Rufus up to the third floor.

The elevator door opens, and with Rufus in my arms, I step off the elevator. Rufus, who is usually pretty sure of himself retreats and watches. Some notice me . . . some notice Rufus . . . some notice Rufus and me, others stare into space. Mom sits before me on the couch with a co-resident.

"Hey, Mom, I brought my dog Rufus to see you . . . do you see Rufus?" I calmly ask, while Rufus clinches my arm.

Mom smiles at me but does not notice Rufus. Some of the other residents notice Rufus and begin to comment on him. I attempt to get Mom to hold her hand out to Rufus. She takes Rufus' paw and gently clenches it. She looks up at me and says, "You're mine, you're mine."

Within moments I realize that she believes she is holding my hand, and Rufus is not part of the picture. She appears to be happy, Rufus is calm, and I accept this moment in time.

Margaret looks over and with a shock in her voice says, "That dog could bite my arm off!"

"Oh, Margaret, Rufus is so gentle he wouldn't harm a fly," I reply, smiling.

"Well, he looks kind of mean to me," she snaps back. Holding Rufus up to Margaret, I suggest that she pet him on his head. Rufus gently licks her hand and she smiles.

Helen looks over at Rufus and alarms the world with, "There's a dog!"

"Yes, Helen, this is Rufus. He's my dog, and I brought him up here to visit everyone," I calmly reply.

"Well, bring him over here so I can see him," she calls out. Rufus takes to Helen and both appear to enjoy each other's company.

One-by-one, I introduce Rufus to the residents of the Carolina Inn. Some are more excited than others. Rufus is not quite sure of these people, so he remains close by my side. The visit proves to be a success and we say our goodbyes.

Chapter Eight

While visiting the beach, Rufus sometimes comes in contact with water. The ocean is unnerving to him and the lake behind Dad's house causes him tension. He senses there is something in the water at both locations—sharks in the ocean and alligators in the lake. Keeping his distance from both bodies is his goal while going on walks.

"Come on, Rufus, let's go check out the ocean," I call to him as I pretty much drag him by his collar along the sand. The closer he gets to the shore, the more apprehensive he becomes. The harsh sounds of the waves crashing cause him to tremble.

"Come on, Rufus . . . it's not really all that bad . . . I wouldn't steer you wrong, little buddy," I attempt to calm him as he digs his claws and paws into the coarse, wet sand. Again, the waves break and the cold, salty water surrounds Rufus' front paws. With a hard jerk of the leash, he takes off in the opposite direction of the ocean.

"Look, Rufus, I don't think you like the ocean much at this time. Maybe next time it will be a little calmer," I say, attempting to reassure him. Wasting little time, Rufus heads for the security of the car.

ALLIGATORS MOVE FROM lake to lake on the golf course behind Dad's house. It is not unusual to see these cold-blooded gators get up to eight-to-ten-foot long before they are captured and relocated. At night, Rufus and I often cut across the golf course in pitch black conditions.

Recently a nine-foot alligator decided to make the lake behind Dad's house his new residence. Luckily, the last few times Rufus and I went on our late evening walk, we did not run into Mr. Gator as he was lake jumping.

Walking down by the lake today, Rufus is a little edgy in the summer heat. There is a quick movement in the water as the long, slender, green alligator slowly surfaces to investigate an unsuspecting Rufus. The Red Irish Terrier is taken aback by the movement and the large body. Of course, having the courage of a lion, he begins to bark to ward off the dangerous intruder.

The alligator watches the little dog patiently then slowly submerges in the dark water. Rufus has protected me and, of course, himself. Wanting to demonstrate to Rufus the power and speed of the alligator, I slowly toss two large oranges into the lake. Immediately, the gator surfaces and with a large open mouth, grabs the orange and bites into it. Rufus watches and slowly backs up, respecting the immense power of this unusual creature.

RUFUS GENERALLY EATS dry dog food. For a treat, I let him sample all sorts of foods. It is strange how he has no taste for shrimp, mussels, oysters, or sushi. Perhaps he knows these food products live in the unknown murky waters that he wants nothing to do with. But when it comes to vegetables and fruits, he has no limits on his appetite. Rabbit, his natural prey, is another tasty food. When the rabbit meat is cooked, Rufus eats it with a passion. His favorite food to date is watermelon salad.

Chapter Nine

Rufus is happy to see me and please me. These are characteristics that I look for in people. Before Rufus came into my life, there was a definite void filled with loneliness. Rufus is now here demonstrating "What can I do for you?" as opposed to "What can I do for him?" Unconditional love perhaps is best illustrated by our pets and how they treat us.

A successful relationship needs to be reciprocating. The blades on a hand saw are designed for cutting forward and a smooth back stroke. The cutting and the resting need to be shared in a relationship. An unequally yoked partnership fails. If there is trouble in the beginning, there will be trouble in the end.

I have two philosophies: People do not change, one learns more about them, and if one has to explain something more than once, he is wasting his time. I apply these thoughts to Rufus and he gets it. He excels.

Rufus never whines for food, water, or to be taken outside. I stay a step ahead of him. Food and fresh water are always in his bowls and four times a day we go for walks. He has toys in sight and hidden around the house. Window blinds are left open for him to see out and Rufus is free to walk anywhere in the house at any time.

This freedom is a result of his behavior and respect for the environment in which he lives. Rufus and I respect each other and the homes we share.

Chapter Ten

Living in a downtown area, Rufus meets other dogs who walk the same beat. Murphy is a black Labrador Retriever who lives in the condominium adjacent to our townhouse. Murphy lives on the second floor and can look off the balcony and watch Rufus enter and exit the back door of the townhouse.

"Hey, Rufus, where are you going today? Are they dragging you off to McCune Technology?" Murphy calls down to Rufus.

"They want me to go out to the building and play with the cat," Rufus calls back.

"A cat . . . why would you want to play with a cat? Those things can scratch you, plus they smell . . . like a litter box," Murphy heckles back.

"Hey, Murphy, you remember the day we met?" Rufus calls back, attempting to change the touchy subject.

"Yeah, I started jumping up and down like I was on a trampoline; it sure gets those humans' attention," Murphy laughs while answering.

"Come on, Murphy, let me see you jump up again . . . come on, Murphy, jump up and down!" Rufus eggs him on. Murphy begins jumping and before long, he is over four foot in the air. "Whoo Hoo." Both Murphy and Rufus continue laughing.

Chapter Eleven

Rufus and I are going to the assisted living facility today. I thought I would take some chocolates to the staff and residents this morning. Rufus quickly runs toward me as I pick up his leash. "Come on, buddy, let's go see Mom," I say to him, snapping the leash on his blue collar. We set off on the short trip and stop by the drugstore to pick up three boxes of chocolate candy.

Like our last visit, Rufus is a little unsure of the assisted living facility. We greet the receptionist, hand her a box of candy, and sign in. We walk down the hallway and are greeted. The patients comment on how well-behaved and cute Rufus is. I press the elevator button and the door opens. Once inside, I look over at Rufus and say, "When the door opens on the third floor, Rufus, that's when the fun begins." Rufus looks up at me not too sure just what is going to happen next. Hesitant, my dog resigns himself to our task at hand.

"Hello, Happy People, I brought some chocolates for you today . . . and look, there's Mom sitting on the couch. Hey, Mom." She glances toward us. Mom recognizes me and begins waving.

"Mom, Rufus and I came to visit you today, and we brought some chocolate candy!" I smile, hoping she will respond to the enthusiasm in my voice.

"You're mine . . . you're mine," she says. Quickly opening the wrapper from the candy, I lift up the box and reveal the assorted chocolates to the residents. The majority notice something new is in the room and begin stirring just a little.

"Here, Mom, you can have the first piece," I say, presenting the box to her. Usually, Mom grabs the first piece and quickly plunks it in her mouth. This day is no different. I circle the room, speaking the residents' names one-by-one and offering the box for them to select a piece of chocolate.

PATTY HAS LIVED on third floor of the assisted living facility for a year and a half. She was diagnosed with dementia/Alzheimer's at the age of forty-five. At fifty-two, Patty is approaching the final stage of the tragic disease Alzheimer's. Her body is twisted and she regresses more and more into the fetal position. A once beautiful and successful woman, she is now becoming more mentally and physically drained as each day passes.

"Patty . . . Patty . . . wake up. I have a piece of candy for you . . . Patty, open your eyes for me," I calmly plead to her. Slowly, her eyes open and she focuses on my face.

"Open up your mouth, Patty, and I will give you a piece of chocolate candy . . . open up wide," I prompt her. Slowly, Patty opens her mouth and I insert part of the chocolate. Gently, she takes a little bite and a slight smile begins to light up her face. Patty looks up at me and says, "Thank you for coming . . . I love you." She takes a few more little bites, continues her soft smile, then falls back into a deep sleep.

RUFUS AND I continue to make the rounds and it proves to be an enjoyable experience. Mom's in good spirits and all is well on the third floor. I have often heard the definition of success is the ability to put a smile on someone's face.

On this sunny Sunday morning, as the elevator door closes on the third floor, Rufus and I are successful. My Red Irish Terrier is learning about humanity the hard way.

Chapter Twelve

While walking on the golf cart path at Sunset Beach, Rufus and I often encounter numerous animals and birds. Today he looks with amazement at the Canadian Geese. The large bird flies, lands, and walks around in a regimented formation.

Next, a lone sandpiper swoops down at Rufus then soars up toward the sky. Rufus takes a running leap and is off to pursue the pesky bird. Not having functioning wings, Rufus quickly lands on his paws and stands upright. The sandpiper swoops down at Rufus again and this time actually makes contact. Rufus lets out a yelp and begins frantically barking at the unruly bird. The Sandpiper screeches louder and finds delight in the challenging quest to upset the four-legged land dweller.

On his next try, Rufus runs a little faster and has a much improved take-off attempt. Still, his flight is short-lived. With a few more loud barks from Rufus, the sandpiper leaves our sight. With our walk complete we head back to the house.

AT DAD'S, RUFUS walks round and round a few times then opts to curl up on the carpet beside the recliner. Before long he is fast asleep, his eyes twitching and his paws moving. He's dreaming, flying, or both.

"The sun is warm today, and I feel great," Rufus thinks as he strolls around on the grass. "It would be nice if Louie or Murphy were here to walk around with me. They would be able to go on a journey."

Suddenly a rabbit darts from behind the bush and I am in rabid pursuit. That rabbit is no match for me . . . then it vanishes. Well that was strange . . . where did it go?

The sky becomes dark then turns red. The pesky sandpiper returns. Strange feelings and uncertainty encompass my thoughts. "What was that . . . that sorry bird has to stop. It is a menace to the community." I growl loudly. I run fast and leap into the air. This time I use my legs and swim through the air. This method works as I gain altitude. Higher and higher I soar, as I set my sights on the sandpiper.

Oh, I'm going to get him . . . I'm going to get you . . . peck on me will you, you silly old bird. Faster and faster . . . closer and closer, then a swat with my paw and down to earth you go, go . . . go . . .

What, what's going on here . . . everything's black and white . . . where's the color!

"Hey Rufus, wake up Rufus . . . do you want a dog biscuit . . . come on, Rufus," Master calls out.

I jump up and look at Master and everything is OK."

Chapter Thirteen

"Hello, is this David McCune?" "Yes."

"This is Doctor Brown's office. Someone has found Rufus," the person the other end of the phone announces.

"What! I didn't know he was missing!" I quickly reply.

"A lawyer in downtown Fayetteville just contacted us. She has Rufus in her office at 300 Hay. Do you know where that is? "Yes, I know. I'm on my way."

How did Rufus get out of the house, I wonder. I know the door was locked. At least he's okay, I tell myself, and in a safe place. On our first visit to the vet, I had a micro chip placed under Rufus' coat and his name is engraved on the back of his rabies tag. That must be how he was identified so fast. I sure am glad my little buddy is safe!

I pull the car into the space in front of my garage door. Sure enough, the backdoor is ajar about four to five inches, just enough room for Rufus to slip out.

I rush around the corner of the townhouse to the law office at 300 Hay Street and look through the window. There is Rufus calmly walking around. As I open the door to the office, Rufus spots me and rushes toward me.

"Hi, I'm Emily." A tall, slender, dark-haired woman approaches us and says softly, "Rufus jumped into my car in the parking lot when I came back from lunch."

"Thank you very much for looking after him. I don't know what I'd do without my little buddy," I say with a broad smile.

"I knew he must live around here and had somehow escaped. I called the vet's number on his rabies tag and I see they didn't waste any time contacting you," she said smiling back.

"Do you have a wish," I eagerly ask. "Whatever you desire . . . what can I do for you?"

"No, I don't need anything. I'm happy to have helped," she replies.

"Again, thanks for finding Rufus and taking care of him," I say in parting, lifting Rufus securely into my arms. I head home to investigate the mysterious lock. How in the world did that door come open? I know for a fact that I locked it when I left for work.

I fiddle with the lock for a few minutes, puzzled. The door is locked, but it opens. The only logical explanation is that the door latch slid out of place when the train came by or some other movement jarred it. The answer is simple: from now on, I will also lock the deadbolt and this will solve my problem. "Come on, Rufus, let's go upstairs and get you something to eat," I say, firmly locking the door and sliding the deadbolt into place.

LATER, HAVING DECIDED that Emily must have some form of reward for her help, I walk over to the Blue Moon Café and purchase a gift certificate for her. It is the least I could do for someone as special as Emily. Her graciousness inspired trust, and I knew that I would eventually consult Emily, as a client, on several legal matters. One never knows what friendships might be forged because of a small, mischievous dog and one simple act of kindness.

Chapter Fourteen

Rufus and I are invited for blueberry pancakes at Diana's home on the Intercoastal Waterway. Graciously accepting the invitation, we set off for the adventure.

After consuming an adequate supply of the delicious pancakes, we begin the long journey down the pier. Rufus, though hesitant, proceeds forward leading the way, carefully walking on the endless treated two-by-sixes. Finally arriving at the end of the pier, Rufus secures himself in a sitting position to watch. The excitement of the Intercoastal Waterway is watching and wondering what is going to sail by next. Jet skis to barges and everything in between sail down the waterways.

"AHOY, MATE, IS that a Red Irish Terrier on the pier there?" a pirate calls out. Rufus, who has never been told of the perils of pirates, begins barking at the boat and the unsavory bunch on board.

"Hey, Little Red, we eat varmint like you so you better respect the likes of us," the one-eyed pirate at the stern calls out.

"Hey, look buddy, you keep your pirate ship to yourself, and I will sit here on the bench on the dock," Rufus calls back with a snicker.

"Hey, Black Jack, pull up along side the dock so I can grab that Red Irish Terrier. I'll make mince meat out of that little dog," Collins calls out to the wheel man.

"Aye mate; let's make some stew out of that dog," Black Jack happily calls back to Collins. The pirate ship pulls up by the dock and three burly pirates quickly board the pier.

"You'll never get me without a fight!" Rufus calls out.

"Grab him boys, don't let him get away. I can tell he's a slippery little varmint," Collins yells. With a mighty leap Rufus jumps off the deck . . . and lands in the water. Collins grabs a net and throws it out at Rufus. Within seconds Rufus becomes entangled in the net and hopelessly sinks. Collins grabs the rope and pulls Rufus on board the pirate ship.

"Ho ho, little fellow, we got you now . . ." Black Jack cackles loudly.

"Boy, have I got myself in a pickle," Rufus thinks. "I'm sure they were just joking about turning me into stew . . . a ship's mascot would be far more appropriate."

"Aye, mate, go fetch me a meat cleaver so I can end this little tramp's sorrowful life," Collins blurts out.

"Hey, buckaroo, who are you calling a tramp!" Rufus snaps Still wrapped up in the cold, wet net, he observes Black Jack has left in search of a meat cleaver. Rufus begins to realize trouble is brewing, and he could be in the pot.

"Look, guys, maybe we could work this out . . . I do happen to know of some buried treasure . . . remember Blackbeard . . . I know where his treasure is hidden."

Black Jack appears with the meat cleaver and is swinging it wildly around. "Dog stew, dog stew," Black Jack yells, while continuing to swing the meat cleaver.

"Bring me the mutt," says Collins.

Collins grabs Rufus and holds him tightly by his back fur. "So you know where Blackbeard's treasure is. Well, you better start talking, and I'll start listening," he yells, pulling a knife up to Rufus's cold, wet neck. Rufus hesitates, then tells his story.

"When I was just a young pup, I ran with some large dogs at the beach. I must admit they were an unsavory bunch. One told me an odd story . . . years ago, a pirate by the name of Blackbeard buried his treasure on a southern island on the Outer Banks of North Carolina. Dogs, enjoying the art of digging, came upon it."

"Dogs do like to dig, so he must be telling the truth," one of the lowly pirates chimes in.

"As I was saying . . . oh, yeah, these dogs were digging, and they came across this old wooden chest. The chest had skull and crossbones on it . . . like the flag on your ship. A huge, rusty lock secured the old wooden chest."

"If the chest was locked how did they know there was treasure in it . . . huh . . . huh?" Collins exclaims as he holds the knife closer to Rufus' neck.

"Because of the lock . . . the lock is to keep everyone out and the gold in."

"So where is this island, and how do we get there?" Collins whispers in Rufus' left ear.

Coming up from the galley, the captain of the vessel appears and yells, "What's going on here . . . what are you doing to that dog?"

"The dog was telling us about a buried treasure," the pirates all join in.

"What? Have you lost your senses, or have you been drinking a little extra rum . . . dogs can't talk," the captain laughs loudly. Realizing this was his chance, Rufus lets out a yelp. Startled, Collins immediately drops him overboard, and Rufus swims back to the dock.

"RUFUS, I MUST have dosed off to sleep; has anything happened while I was napping?" I ask with a yawn. Rufus looks up and rolls his eyes, if he only knew . . .

"Hey, Rufus, look at this old boat headed our way . . . sort of looks like an old pirate ship," I say with a smile.

Chapter Fifteen

David Junior is a cat person, and Lucy is David's cat. She frets over him when his is out of town. When David was a senior in high school and living at the beach house on Ocean Isle Beach, Sarah and I decided to surprise him with a dog. Sarah and I were riding around in the beach area and stumbled on a sign that read: "Dalmatian Puppies for Sale." Naive to the non-stop energy of the Dalmatian breed, we stop to check it out. The mother is big . . . the father is bigger, and the pups are small, cuddly and cute. Both of us being a little short-sighted, we opt to purchase a little Dalmatian puppy and surprise David.

After playing with the pup and tiring him out, we place him on David's pillow and tuck him in with the covers. As expected, young David is happy and excited to find the pup and names him "Chip."

Chip grew, and grew, and continued to grow. Being a senior in high school, David's life and schedule did not incorporate much time for Chip. Because of his rambunctious nature and size, Chip lived in a caged area under the beach house. He became a prisoner in a six-foot-square space. His joy in life was opening the gate and letting himself run free. Time passed, and Chip's life became fixed.

One day I had a brilliant idea! I would take Chip to McCune Technology and he could live there and run free throughout the buildings and play on the six acres of grass. After about a week of this madness, one of the employees asked if he could take Chip to live on his farm. Without hesitation, I helped load Chip and his large bag of dog food into the employee's car.

Years later, during a family conversation about Chip one evening, David asked, "Why didn't you and Sarah bring home a kitten? Cats are a lot less trouble than a dog."

Chapter Sixteen

May I introduce Lucy, David Jr.'s cat. She is a feral cat that found us. Lucy is rather large with long, jet-black hair. She lives at McCune Technology. Lucy has never been around animals except for Louie and Rufus. Louie did not fare well when introduced to Lucy. Within minutes, Lucy's sharp, extended claws scratched Louie's soft, pink, sensitive nose. He quickly learned to keep his distance from Lucy when visiting McCune Technology.

On Rufus' first visit to McCune Technology, he was but a wee thing. His instincts led him to keep his distance from the big, black, long-haired feline with the wild eyes. Months later Rufus and Lucy became pretty close in size. She tolerates him. He likes to sneak up behind Lucy and pounce on her. Occasionally they will lie down together or, on true special moments, touch their noses. Two lost souls on an island.

"Hi, Lucy. Anything special going down today?" Rufus says, smiling as he enters the front door.

"Rufus, I thought you were guarding the house . . . why are you here ?" asks Lucy.

Rufus ignores her and runs back to the lab to see if any toys are to be found. "Oh good! A sock. I found a sock, and it appears to be a stinky sock at that," Rufus enthusiastically calls out while tossing the sock up in the air.

"Rufus, that's just nasty; you should know better than to chew on a sock . . . one never knows where that sock as been." Lucy replies with a look of stinging disgust.

"Louie was telling me about one of his buddies who swallowed a hole tube stock, and when he dumped, they had to pull it out . . . I heard it got sort of hung up on something . . . now that's a stinky sock, Lucy," Rufus laughs and continues to chew.

"You know, Rufus, when humans refer to each other as dogs, I know where the phrase comes from now," Lucy replies heading back to the front office and shaking her head.

Chapter Seventeen

My friend Klara lives in Connecticut. Numerous people, including me, had suggested that she should get a dog. A dog rescue unit from Atlanta visited her town and brought with them twenty-four dogs for the residents to adopt.

The story told was these dogs came from families in the local Atlanta area who had recently lost their job. Due to housing dilemmas, they were forced to give up their beloved pets. Small, medium, and large dogs of various breeds were on display and ready for adoption. Klara decided on a Rat Terrier with the name Hugo.

Klara is very independent and she likes everything in order. Both Hugo and Klara began to adapt to each other and Klara was very excited about her new four-legged friend. We often told each other dog stories. Hugo was the apple of her eye and she showed him off to all who met him. As long as Klara was within sight, all was good in Hugo's world.

In the beginning, Klara brought Hugo to work with her. As time passed, she felt he was ready to be left alone. She left him on the porch and he did a little damage. She brought Hugo back to work.

Some suggested she should crate him. She crated him, left for work and returned at lunch. Upon her return, she discovered Hugo had escaped from the crate and Klara decided to rename him Houdini. She later just called him Huey.

KLARA HAS A fear of mice. Being a Rat Terrier, Huey should be excellent for clearing her residence and yard of mice. Klara and her niece were preparing the storage building beside her house for winter and Huey was busy watching and sniffing.

Suddenly, a mouse appeared and Klara screamed. Huey ran and he continued to run until he found a safe place to hide. I believe this was a turning point in their relationship.

IT WAS TIME to return to work after a long weekend and Klara left Huey in the crate. This time she also secured it with numerous twist ties. Upon her return, she found that Huey had pulled another Houdini and escaped the crate and twist ties. Damage total . . . . ding, ding, ding—$500—plus urine was everywhere.

The next day Klara borrowed a larger crate and secured it this time with a padlock. Huey stared at her when she left. Houdini returns. Total damage . . . . ding, ding, ding—$500—and more urine in places Klara couldn't figure out how it got there.

"Dog's got to go . . . he disrespected me. I can't take this anymore. He has separation issues, and this is not going to work . . . I can't deal with this anymore," Klara told me in a very concerned demeanor. Attempting to comfort her, I actually couldn't think of anything to say. She had a dog that disrespected her.

Klara contacted the pet adoption organization and informed them of her dilemma. They were shocked that little Hugo could cause such mental and physical distress in Klara's happy world. She told them they could have Hugo back, and she was ready to move on.

Prior to the pickup of Hugo, Klara's niece and her boyfriend decided to take Hugo. They hoped to change his behavior and provide for him.

In the meantime, Klara is repairing the damage, and her blood pressure has gone down. This winter, once again, she will be setting traps for the mice.

Chapter Eighteen

The stuffed furry brown rabbit Rufus leaves at the beach is in need of eye surgery. Over time and some hard play, Rufus' life-like rabbit is missing an eye. Besides this injury, his furry friend is holding up, but Rufus is pulling the stuffing out through the rabbit's empty eye socket.

LaRhonda, Dad's caregiver, is asked to mend the torn area in the eye opening. All knew the tedious surgery will not bring the eye back. Agreeing to our request, LaRhonda painstakingly places the necessary stitches in the injured bunny.

Rufus sits and patiently watches LaRhonda sew up his little friend. The operation is complete, and LaRhonda sits the happy bunny on the floor. Rufus grabs his baby and quickly runs through the house. Before long he lies down with his baby close by.

"Hey, Rufus. Let's go for a walk," I call for him, as I search for the leash. Opening the door, I quickly notice Rufus is holding the rabbit in his mouth. Apparently, he is going to take his baby on the walk. "OK, Rufus, if you take your baby, you have to carry it the whole time," I inform him. Since the rabbit is held securely in Rufus' teeth, he unable to answer . . . he appears to mutter something, and his head nods.

On his usual mile walk on the golf cart path, Rufus drops the rabbit a few times then sternly picks it up. Being careful not to mark his rabbit, Rufus carefully places it on the ground, takes a few steps, then relieves himself. On the return trip back to Dad's house, Rufus drops the rabbit and continues on.

"Rufus, you better grab your baby or you may never see him again," I suggest. Immediately, Rufus retreats to where he dropped his baby, grabs it in his mouth and shakes it a few times. We quickly cross over the fairway to avoid interrupting play as we return to the house. A foursome is searching for their golf balls, and the players observe Rufus.

"Hey, what does that dog have in its mouth?" a golfer who has already located his ball calls to me.

"It's his stuffed rabbit . . . he's getting ready for hunting season," I laugh, answering him.

"Well it certainly looks real," he exclaims. Back in the house, Rufus jumps up on the bed, carefully places his baby on a pillow, and returns to the sun room to see if anything is going on.

Chapter Nineteen

On our return to Fayetteville, Rufus and I take our usual walk downtown to Festival Park and stop by the Blue Moon Café for some watermelon salad. Being within health code compliance, we choose outdoor seating. Daisy sees us sitting and comes through the open door.

"Hi, Rufus, how are you doing today?" she politely asks.

"He's doing pretty well today. We had a great time at the beach and decided to stop by and have some watermelon salad," I reply. "If you would, please split a serving and place it in two to-go cups,"

"No problem," Daisy say happily. Before long, our watermelon salad arrives in two identical half-quart Styrofoam containers. Knowing how we both enjoy watermelon salad, the chef has given us quite a bit extra. Daisy places Rufus' bowl beside him on the ground and places mine on the table in front of me.

"Thanks, Daisy. You know . . . in Paris it is acceptable for dogs to sit in the chairs at outside cafés. I don't believe the health department around here could accept this," I laugh.

"I am usually scared of dogs, but I really like Rufus," Daisy says. Rufus notices we both have food and he jumps up at the table to examine what I am eating. Satisfied that we both have the same food, he quickly returns to his bowl. Rufus consumes all of his watermelon salad and licks the bowl clean. Now he is staring at me and knows food is still in my bowl.

"Daisy, I guess I'll give him some more of mine. I would hate to see him go hungry," I say, laughing. I carefully pour some of my salad into Rufus' licked-clean bowl. Not hesitating, I empty all the succulent juice from my container into his. Joyfully, Rufus laps up everything in his bowl.

Finished with our lunch, Rufus and I say our goodbyes to Daisy and head home. About fifty feet into the walk, Rufus is hit with an unforeseen moving experience. I quickly cover his golden nuggets with some freshly-laid shredded wood bark. Back at the townhouse, I bid Rufus farewell and return to work.

WHEN I RETURN home, Rufus is glad see me, and we go for our usual walk to Festival Park. Completing his business, Rufus and I return home. Later that night, I retire to bed. All of a sudden, to my surprise, my feet are sensing something cold and wet.

"Rufus, did you have an accident on my bed?" I sternly question him. Without hesitation, he jumps off the dry side and sheepishly slides underneath the bed. With the bedding removed and mattress cleaned, I find a dry bed in another bedroom. Eventually, Rufus crawls out from hiding place and comes to sleep on the floor beside me.

I know it is completely out of Rufus' character to soil the house. Analyzing the outcome of the mysterious urine, the new variable to the equation is . . . an abundance of watermelon salad.

Months earlier, the family was vacationing on Jekyll Island, Georgia. Prior to going to sleep, I had quickly consumed either three or four martinis. Sometime in the night, my kegel muscle completely relaxed and, sure enough, I had a major urine spill. First time this had happened since my terrible two's. The variable . . . an abundance of alcohol prior to sleep.

Rufus must have gone up to the bedroom on the third floor for a catnap after consuming the watermelon salad. In a sound sleep, with an abundance of liquid in his digestive tract, Rufus' kegel muscle relaxed, and his flood came forth.

Chapter Twenty

Rufus enjoys walks and meeting new dogs and human friends. Funny, how he sniffs dogs and licks people. Dogs must have an irresistible smell and humans a good taste.

It would be nice if Rufus could accompany me on a walk without the need of his secure leash. Without shackles a prisoner can escape and without a leash, Rufus would chase movement to the ends of the earth.

On our usual early morning walks to Festival Park in Downtown Fayetteville, we meet many people. Odds are we find a homeless person or discover a body. In the meantime, we will just walk and see what happens next.

"That's the cutest dog I have ever seen. What's her name?" the girl with a book bag, wearing the Pembroke University sweatshirt, asks.

"Well, actually, he is a boy dog and his name is Rufus," I answer, quickly correcting her.

"Well, he is the most beautiful dog I have ever seen," she says, patting Rufus.

"He's Rufus the Wonder Dog," I proudly inform her. "You see this retractable leash he's attached to . . . well he can soar like a kite. Would you like to see him fly?" I ask.

"Sure, I've never seen a dog fly, and I have never seen a dog like Mister Rufus, either," she exclaims with a sense of curiosity.

"Please don't tell anyone because the press will find out, and it will surely lead to chaos," I politely ask her. She promises that she will tell no one and will not record anything on her cell phone. I had not even thought of her recording Rufus on her cell phone, so I know she must be trustworthy.

"OK, Rufus, go ahead and fly for just a few minutes. But stay sort of low, and if you see anyone, land immediately." I spend quite a bit of time talking with Rufus because his listening skills are very keen. Round and round Rufus runs in a circle as I let out the retractable leash. And then, like magic, he lifts up off the ground. The girl's eyes open wider and the look of surprise on her face takes one back. Rufus, now fifteen foot off the ground, is soaring around us at tremendous speed.

"How do you like his flying skills?" I ask. "You know, I really thought you were joking . . . I never saw a dog fly before. How does he do it . . . just how is that dog flying?" she asks.

"You have heard of a flying squirrel, right?" She nods her head in agreement, staring at Rufus going round and round. "I've had numerous biology and science classes in college, and the professors never taught us anything like this.

Mister . . . you have a flying dog. That's just not normal," she exclaims, attempting to convince herself.

"Anyway, see how there is an open cavity under his body . . . he traps air, creates lift. Quick speed is the propulsion . . . that equals thrust. It's the same principle as an airplane."

"Well, that's got to be the neatest thing I have ever seen," she says, laughing as she wipes the perspiration from her forehead.

"Go ahead and come in for a landing, Rufus," I call up to him. Without hesitation, Rufus lifts up his ears as flaps and begins his dissent. As usual, his landing is superb, and he walks over to us.

"Well, Mister Rufus, I have never seen anything as amazing as your flying. Thanks for that excellent demonstration," the girl says, smiling. She thanked us again and departed.

Chapter Twenty-One

While cleaning the house and vacuuming, I discover something unusual: the townhouse is exceptionally clean. The hardwood floors, tile, and carpet are free of debris. Then, I realize what happens.

Dad and I go out to dinner Saturday night. My friend Alexis is working at the chosen establishment and we sit in her area. I tell her about the townhouse and how the floors stay immaculate. Rufus, in his complete satisfaction to please and feel useful, gobbles up everything on the floors and disposes them outside.

"I think you should change his name to Hoover," Alexis happily suggests. We all laugh.

AS IT RELATES to Rufus's schedule of disposal, he urinates three times a day and defecates two times a day. Keep in mind he only eats two small bowls of food a day. When we go for walks he opens up his herbivore/carnivore mindset and consumes some form of plant or insect life every few feet. Between what he eats inside and outside the house, this makes up half of his daily diet.

From a cost standpoint, Rufus is an excellent asset to the household, plus a great friend and a true gem to be around.

Chapter Twenty-Two

Dad has complained lately about his back hurting. At eighty-four, it is understandable he should have some pain in his old age. Of course, he does not see himself as old or elderly. He views himself as an adult. Dad's back has ached throughout the morning. I suggest he lie down flat on his back and perhaps take a nap while I run some errands.

On my return, Dad tells me how Rufus had curled up beside him in the bed. I check Dad's back and decide to place some towel-wrapped ice on the discomforting area for fifteen minutes. As I position the towel against the tender area on Dad's back, Rufus notices the activity and comes over. He gently licks the spot on Dad's back where he senses the discomfort and then promptly lies down beside the inflamed area. When I leave the room, Rufus stays close beside Dad instead of following me.

Rufus loves his Grandpa, and Grandpa loves Rufus. Giving comfort is a gift.

Chapter Twenty-Three

Darkness replaces the bright sunny day as Rufus drifts off into a sound sleep. Stretched out on his back on the couch in the sun room, Rufus props his head on a pillow and his mouth is wide open. After a long day of guarding the home he takes it easy. A slight rustling is heard and Rufus immediately resumes his guard position and stance. Sounding his alarm, he repeatedly barks to let all know Rufus is on duty.

"Come on, Rufus, go back to sleep. There is nothing outside that's going to bother us," I assuredly state. Not relinquishing his post, Rufus continues the frantic barks.

"Come on, Rufus, enough is enough. There is nothing out there," I say, hoping his yapping will subside. As he continues to bark, I decide to open the door and show him there's nothing on the other side of the door to harm us. As I open the door Rufus lunges, escaping into the darkness.

And there, on the back deck, lies the alligator. Rufus continues to bark as the big gator opens his wide mouth and hisses. Not knowing what to think of all this commotion, Dad ventures over to the open door. "Well, that's an alligator out there. We need to close the door before he decides to come inside," Dad calmly says as he steps back a few feet. Again, the gator snarls and suggests we leave his turf.

Moments later, I realize Rufus is not around me and the alligator is looking in the opposite direction of us. A surge of movement and the alligator is on the move. The darkness of night prevents us from locating Rufus and I panic, knowing a dog Rufus' size would be a mere snack for a hungry gator. We hear a splash in the water and the sound of thrashing, and Rufus is nowhere to be heard or seen. "Rufus . . . Rufus. Rufus, come here, boy . . . Rufus!" I repeatedly call. Silence echoes in the still, starless night.

Out of the darkness, Rufus suddenly emerges and scurries in the door. "Rufus where have you been? I was worried to death that something might have happened to you!" I rejoice. Rufus is damp and trembling. He licks me a few times, shakes off some of the water on his coat, and jumps up on the couch.

We are not sure what happened to the alligator or Rufus that chilly, dark night. Maybe Rufus ran out the door hoping he would distract the alligator. Or, he ran out of the house because the alligator was on the way in and he didn't want to be gobbled up. These are the mysteries to life we will never know.

Chapter Twenty-Four

Wanting to get a quick bite to eat, I walk across the street to the Blue Moon. I admit it is nice living in the downtown and being able to walk to a restaurant. On the way back home after lunch, I find a bright yellow tennis ball. Since there are no tennis courts around, I assume it has fallen from the sky and is fair game.

As I near home, I see Rufus at the back door of the townhouse frantically waving at me. Sure to reciprocate his gesture, I enthusiastically wave back. This seems to get him more excited. "Yay, Master is home," Rufus barks.

Once in the house, I show him the amazing ball and toss it down the hall. Rufus takes off after his new, round, furry friend. Now, with the ball in his mouth, Rufus runs upstairs. Confident that I am not going to take back his temporary prized procession, he releases the tight grip and appears to examine the fuzzy object.

Rufus has never seen a ball before. It has no eyes, no tail, and no stuffing. He and I both find this odd because a ball is commonly a dog's first toy. Moving beyond this thought, we both work on the throw and return game. He likes this play activity and is a little hesitant on giving the ball back. After a few more tosses, he becomes bored and finds his toy beaver to play with.

RUFUS AND I leave to visit Dad at the beach for a few days. Upon our return, Rufus finds the ball on the second floor. He starts throwing it up in the air and watching it bounce.

In the meantime his friend, the beaver, patiently watches the whimsical play. The silent beaver knows that ball will soon be forgotten, and Rufus will be sleeping with and feeding him in no time at all.

Chapter Twenty-Five

Upon quickly exiting McCune Technology, Rufus observes an unknown movement in the bush beside the door. Diving into the sharp, prickly bush results in the exodus of his moving discovery: a large praying mantis. Jumping into the tall green grass, its camouflage cover is successfully achieved.

Rufus begins sniffing and moving rapidly about. Suddenly, he locates his prey. The praying mantis lifts up his hind legs and hisses. Rufus licks the insect and a bad taste enters his sensitive mouth. Not wanting Rufus to cause damage, I drag him off to the woods, but time and distance will not erased Rufus' desire to capture the praying mantis.

Lucy is outside walking around the garden. Rufus spots her and begins a slow stride toward her. Ever so gently and cautiously, he stalks Lucy. Then, without notice, he pounces on her. Feeling step one of his quest is complete, Rufus firmly pulls me back to the location of the praying mantis. I spot the bug quickly, but Rufus can't see it. After a few prompts, points, and commands, he finally locates his victim. Rufus gently swats at it with his paw and the praying mantis rears up and hisses. Rufus barks and the praying mantis hisses.

This continues for a few moments until I pull Rufus away.

Now inside the building, Rufus wants out. Time passes as Rufus stares out the window. Finally, we are ready to leave and he shoots out the door. The praying mantis is nowhere to be found.

Chapter Twenty-Six

This morning Rufus and I awoke to a little added noise in downtown Fayetteville. Today is the International Folk Festival. At an early seven-o'clock on Saturday morning, we set out for our usual walk to Festival Park. Instead of being the only ones on the journey, we are surrounded with new people and a flurry of activities. Everyone is working frantically to set up their booths to make ready for the thousands of soon-to-be onlookers and customers.

Rufus is taken back by all of the movement and the surplus of people. Workers and vendors from all cultures are cooking foods from around the world. As we pass some cultures from the Orient, the vendors look at Rufus and begin to point. Knowing it is common to prepare and cook cats and dogs, I move Rufus away from their booth. Rufus, feeling a little uneasy at their stares, happily obliges, as I pull forward toward home.

"Hi, little fellow," a young girl in the Arts Council booth greets Rufus. Standing on his hind legs, Rufus holds his paw out for her to shake. Not expecting this reaction, she freezes up momentarily then graciously extends her hand. He gently licks her hand a few times then sits before her.

"What kind of dog is he . . . I have never seen a dog that color before?" she inquisitively asks.

"Rufus is a Red Irish Terrier, and he can also fly . . . that's why I keep him on a leash. I would let him demonstrate his gift, but there are too many people around at this time," I proudly respond.

"I attend Pembroke University, and I heard a girl talking the other day about a flying dog . . . come to think about it, she said it was in Fayetteville at Festival Park," she exclaims with a very profound look on her face. Realizing I had said a little too much and a crowd was gathering, we quickly say our goodbyes and depart.

ON OUR NEXT walk, Rufus has no desire to return to Festival Park. Perhaps he wants no part of "becoming Rufus on a stick." When we head in that direction, Rufus protests by placing his behind in the sitting position and won't move. Deciding not to drag him, I suggest he lead the way and I will follow. Before long, we arrive at the Blue Moon Café and Rufus greets his friends, Daisy and Lea. After a short visit, Rufus is ready to return to the sanctuary of the townhouse and leads me home.

NOW IT'S TIME for Dad and me to venture down to Festival Park and partake in some of the international cuisine. Fighting our way through the crowd, we come upon the Philippine vendors. Their varieties of foods look and smell favorable, so we order two combination platters and tea. With nowhere to sit and eat in sight, Dad and I carry our food back to the townhouse, even though we must walk through a sea of moving bodies. Rufus is happy we have returned and is excited to see we have food with us.

"David, when your mother and I were in the Philippines, we were walking around the market and one could pick out puppies and kittens," Dad says. Knowing where this story was going, because I had heard it before, and was concerned that Rufus would hear the ill fate of those in the Philippines, I chose not to comment. The rice is good. The egg roll is good. The noodles are good, and the meat is on a stick. Not sure of the meat's natural origin, I feel it is best to let Rufus eat some of the noodles and rice. It was probably goat, after all.

After lunch, Dad is ready to return to the beach. As we close the door to the townhouse, Rufus quickly runs to the car and jumps in. The festival proved to be a little to much for him, and he is ready to see his rabbit.

Chapter Twenty-Seven

Both Dad and Rufus are happy to be back at Sunset Beach. Rufus runs into the house and searches for his rabbit. The little bunny is nowhere to be found. Rufus begins jumping and pulling on me. "OK, Rufus, I'll help you find your bunny rabbit," I respond, looking around. Room by room, Rufus and I search for his lost friend.

"Rufus, did you hide the rabbit before we left?" I ask. Not sure, he looks up and shakes his head back and forth, left to right. As we continue searching, I spot the rabbit under a throw pillow on the bed. I grab it and toss it on the floor. Happy now, Rufus tosses it up and down. Rabbit! Rabbit!

RUFUS NEEDS TO make a final pit stop before going to bed. As expected, a short, quick walk is not on his agenda. Suddenly, four very huge objects dart out from behind a house. Rufus looks to his right while a buck, a doe, and two fawns run through the yards. Not sure if he should be in the fight or flight mode, Rufus stands up on his hind legs and starts chasing the deer down the street. His balance is superb, as I follow the leash and him on this action-packed pursuit.

Eventually, the deer family vanishes into the woods and Rufus returns to all fours and sniffs the ground where the deer have tracked. Shaking his head, he glares at me. Once again the dreaded leash has held him back from the fulfillment of adventure.

Chapter Twenty-Eight

Rufus should be a year old now. Not knowing his true birth date is an obstacle in celebrating my little buddy's birthday. No known birthday and an orphan, the little waif shows me and others unconditional love.

Often at night, before drifting off to sleep, I place my hand on Rufus and pray. I thank God for our family, friends, the people we come in contact with, and the business.

A surrogate is a noun that is defined as one that takes the place of another, a substitute. Rufus acts as a surrogate for me, and perhaps I act as a surrogate for him.

Chapter Twenty-Nine

Snif . . . snif . . . . snif . . . snif . . . sniiiiiiiiiif . . . . ah . . . that feels sooo gooood . . . . woooh. I'm outside, outside having a good time.

"Rufus, that's a good buddy . . . you're part of the good buddy system," my master calls out. I wish he would come up with another line. He thinks it's cute. I often wonder whose trick this is . . . his or mine. I like being around him and the others in our pack. Big building ahead and then the field. Outside has lots of smells. I love to smell, all the scents of a rainbow.

BACK HOME NOW and off the leash, like I'm going to make a break for it. He is just too overprotective. Master forgets I hear and sense time fast.

Come on skunk, let's go upstairs. This is my favorite part of the day. Master has a cup of coffee; I can just relax and watch him before he leaves. Skunk, come on let's see what Squirrel's up too. Ready, set, run . . . jump . . . pounce . . . got you again, squirrel, you never saw me coming.

Beaver was my first baby. Well that's what master calls them. They are my cubs, and I give them space. Beaver . . . now where is Beaver?

There he is in the basket. Master's cub Sarah cleaned the burrow and placed my cubs in the basket. She also removed scents throughout burrow.

Beaver, its time to eat; lets go to the food bowl. Plop. You stay here and eat while I play with skunk and squirrel. It sounds like master is getting ready for work, so I need to go upstairs and check on him. The two of you entertain each other.

There he is in the rain box. He will be coming out soon. Well . . . in the meantime I will just lie down and wait. Ah, nothing better than a great stretch. I like the grass in the bathroom; it feels so good. Sounds like the rain stopped. Master's out, master's out; I need to help dry him off. Maybe someday he will learn how to shake.

"Come on, Rufus, let's go downstairs. I need to get to work," Master says, patting my head. Down the stairs we go. Master opens the door and tells me good-bye as he carefully closes the door behind him and then locks it.

Now we're going to have some fun. With a leap, I lift up and fly up the stairs. Landing beside Squirrel and Skunk, I catch them both off guard and they startle just a little. Come on guys, let's go see if Beaver left anything in the bowl. Beaver, finish up, we're on the way!

A full belly is the best . . . right guys? Let's take a nap. OK, Skunk, you take the first floor. Beaver, you take the second floor, and Squirrel, well, you and I will take lookout on the third floor. Guys, let's take your positions. Squirrel, jump on my back and hold on. Clear the runway, "Rufus to tower, Rufus to tower! Come in tower."

"Tower to Rufus, you are cleared for take off."

"Hold on tight, Squirrel, we're taking off!

Turn one coming up. Turn two coming up. Squirrel, I didn't lose you back there, did I? Turn three coming up. Turn four coming up."

"Rufus, this is third floor tour; you are cleared for landing, I repeat you are cleared for landing."

"Hold on, Squirrel, we're coming in hot."

'*Bump.*' That's kind of hard on my paws. "Squirrel, you take Master's front bedroom, and I'll take the rear. Remember, when master is gone, the burrow is our responsibility, and we must defend it from intruders."

"Bark . . . bark . . . bark . . . jump, bark, bark, bark, unfamiliar noise outside boys. Sound the alarm! Sound the alarm! Everyone man your positions; I'm going down to investigate. Cubs, there are strangers out in the parking lot at the rear of the burrow. I'm continuing to bark to let them know we mean business. Sniff . . . sniff . . . oh yeah, I can smell them now. They have a scent from an unfamiliar pack. Yep, they are leaving in a transporter. We scared them away cubs, now everyone back to your positions. Again, cubs, let me say . . . job well done."

MASTER'S HOME, MASTER'S home. I need to get to the back door before he unlocks it. Run, jump and fly . . . . coming in for a landing . . . swoop, and another great landing. There he is! There he is! It's my Master.

"Hey, Rufus. Hey little buddy, I'll bet you're ready to go outside," Master says, securing me to the leash. Jump, jump, jump . . . I'm, so happy to see you, and our burrow is secure.

Chapter Thirty

"Come on, Rufus let's go on the final walk this evening," I say, securing him to his leash. It's a wet, cold, dreary night and I hope his outside journey will be swift. With his long coat, Rufus is not bothered by the inclement weather, but before long he demonstrates he's ready to head home.

On the way back to our townhouse, we stop at the main intersection and I press the pedestrian crossing button. The pedestrian crossing light flashes and we safely proceed. Half-way through the intersection, a car parallel to the crosswalk makes a speedy abrupt turn and is headed straight toward me. Rufus, fifteen feet in front leading the way, is safe.

I have some quick decisions to make: One, I can pull Rufus back—this will result in Rufus being hit. Two, I can drop the retractable leash, and Rufus will panic. Third, I can jump in front of the car that is headed between Rufus and me. Quickly making my choice, I opt to jump in front of the car.

Successfully completing my rescue of Rufus, I make a motion to the driver of the car. With an ignorant look, he stops his car and rolls down his driver's side window.

"You need to pay attention!" I inform him. "I didn't see you," he replies.

"You need to pay attention!" I say louder and stronger.

"I'm watching, I'm watching," he says in a somewhat shaky voice.

"You need to pay attention!" I say for the third time. He rolls his window up and speeds away.

"So the guy didn't see us, Rufus . . . why did he run the light?" I ask, a bit confused. "Come on, Rufus, let's check something out . . . I assume that when we push the crosswalk button, and the pedestrian light comes on, that all stop lights are red," I say to him, back tracking to the pedestrian light button.

"OK, Rufus let's check this out," I add, pushing the safety button. "The pedestrian light is on, and the stoplight running parallel to the crosswalk is green!" I observe. "Well, Rufus that explains a lot!" I tell him, making a mental note to call the City Engineering in the morning and report the malfunction.

MY CONVERSATION WITH the City Engineering Department the next day is enlightening. A federal law mandates that traffic lights running parallel to crosswalks are to illuminate green during the illumination of the crosswalk light. It is the responsibility of the operator of the motor vehicle to watch for pedestrians in the crosswalk and not to run into them.

This new-found information is shocking. I ask the inspector about the consequences for sight and physically challenged individuals. He again states it is the responsibility of the operator of the motor vehicle to watch for pedestrians in the crosswalks.

Following my conversation with the inspector, I decide to research the subject on the internet. It turns out, half of all pedestrian accidents and fatalities happen in pedestrian crosswalks. Now, when I walk Rufus in pedestrian crosswalks, I pay closer attention to the surrounding motor vehicles.

Chapter Thirty-One

I wonder when Master will return to the burrow. I miss him. I am so happy when he returns from the work hive. Master and David act different there. They don't play there . . . except when Master beats his drums. He appears to be happy then. I worry about him when he is not near me. I listen to him talk with the pack and he seems pulled in all directions. I never want him to feel like I am pulling him.

I sense when he wakes up in the night. I can feel his mind racing. Immediately, I come to his rescue and place my head on his chest and he drifts back to sleep. I have a purpose in serving Master and he knows I do a great job. I am very lucky to have a nice master and be part of a wonderful, loving pack.

He's back! Master's back! I hear his car and he will be opening the door soon. Happy dance, I'm doing the happy dance . . . happy dance, shake, shake, shake.

"Come on, Rufus, get down . . . let's put your leash on so we can go for a walk," Master says, patting me on the head. If Master would do a happy dance, I bet he would feel better. Maybe someday he will join in. Let's see, I'm going to take Raccoon with me.

"Rufus, are you sure you want to take the raccoon with you? We're going on a long walk, and you often tire when you carry your baby." Master reminds me, knowing that eventually my baby will end up in his pocket.

Master's right, Raccoon, you stay here and keep an eye on things. Master and I will return soon.

"OK, Rufus, lets go. I'm glad you decided to leave your baby," Master says, closing and locking the door.

I WISH I could talk like the others in the pack. I have so many ideas and thoughts I can share. I have studied the computer at the work hive and believe this may be the tool. So many questions I need answered. I am a good listener. Master goes on and on sometimes and I just listen and listen. Enough of this; we are on a walk and I just need to enjoy sniffing.

Dog ahead, dog ahead . . . need tooooo go seeeee the dog, Master! Sniff . . . sniff. Hey, you smell pretty good! You must have been places. Sniff, sniff. I sure like my dog friends. It's never a long visit but a good one, sort of like they are passing you by . . .

"Rufus you're the best!" Master says, looking over at me. "You're the reason for the walks we take throughout the day. I enjoy the walks.

Walking with you is a great escape from the toils of the day. And I'm sure you enjoy the walks as well."

Chapter Thirty-Two

Back at Sunset Beach, Rufus is ready to go out for a walk. Knowing that he recently put forth number two, we are free to walk in the neighborhood without reserve. In no time Rufus delivers an encore performance of number two. As Rufus takes mark, the home owner assumes the bird dog position. As soon as Rufus completes his business, the homeowner comes over to investigate.

"Are you planning on cleaning up after your dog?" He asks with authority.

"Actually, Rufus eats bio-degradable dog food that begins breaking down when it comes within the presence of oxygen. I'm sure you have noticed other pet owners who remove the waste with plastic bags. Landfills across the country are riddled with plastic bags containing dog poop. The methane gas produced from this containment process is assisting in the destruction of our ozone layer. Rufus and I are both green. By tomorrow morning the golden nuggets will be gone, and the resulting fertilizer will be spreading throughout your lawn" I tell him with authority.

The man has a very puzzled look on his face and asks, "You mean to tell me that stuff is going to be gone in the morning?"

Realizing that he had missed my previous statements I simply answered, "Yes." He looks at me, shakes his head up and down and walks away.

LATER THAT NIGHT, Rufus and I venture in the direction of the decomposing feces. Suddenly, a flashlight beam appears, pointed at the lawn ahead. As we approach, I realize the home owner is searching for the poop.

"It's gone isn't it?" I ask.

"Where did it go?" He is more puzzled than ever.

"Greatest dog food on the market, wouldn't you say?"

"That's amazing, just amazing. Bring your dog by any time . . . and thanks," he says, smiling at Rufus.

Chapter Thirty-Three

I sit on a white leather club chair on the third floor bedroom and look at Rufus. He is a true pleasure to be around. Fish, Raccoon, Squirrel, and Beaver are up here with us. I'm not quite sure where he left Skunk. More than likely Skunk is down on the first floor standing guard.

At the moment Rufus is playing with Fish, tossing it up and down and squeezing it for the full sounds. Squeak, squeak . . . squeak, squeak, squeak. He entertains himself well.

Before long Rufus is fast asleep. I hear a rustling noise and he springs into action. Barking rabidly, Rufus makes his way to the first floor. After checking the front and rear perimeters, he feels everything is safe and returns to a restful position.

David Jr. joins us and teases Rufus by placing Squirrel on the top rail of the canopy bed. After a few jumps and misses, Rufus picks up a pillow and throws it toward his cub, hoping to knock it down. I watch with amazement at how he is using a tool to accomplish a task. After numerous unsuccessful attempts, I gently lift his Squirrel from its peril and place it in Rufus' happy mouth. As expected, he rejoices and gives it a good, strong squeak.

THE EVENING COMES to an end, and Rufus is ready for his final walk. Often he takes his paw or paws and grasps at me, pulling my hand toward him. I follow, and he lets me know his desire.

"Come on, Rufus, let's go for a walk and see what the outside brings," I say, with a laugh. Not wasting any time, he runs downstairs with anticipation, races out the open door, and quickly heads to the left in the direction of the old Fayetteville train station museum. On our leisurely walks, I reflect on the day and relax as we explore what's ahead. We never know with whom we will cross paths.

Chapter Thirty-Four

A word to describe Rufus is "enthusiasm." He demonstrates a true joy in every activity. This attribute in his personality leads me to realize what is missing in my life. The opposite of enthusiasm is depression. Depression and disappointment are emotions I struggle with. As I watch Rufus and the true joy in life he displays, I understand what my soul longs for.

One of my latest endeavors is "Dancing with the Fayetteville Stars." As my partner Sunday and I practice our routine, her daughter Terra observes. When we're finished, I ask Terra, "What can we do to improve?"

Without reservation she replies, "You could smile."

I am showing no enthusiasm. Actually, I am looking at this choreographed dance as an additional stress on my life. I quickly realize: I volunteered for this event and I should be enjoying the entire experience. Everything is positive and I am turning it negative. I am the one with the problem! I am the one who is looking at this as drudgery! I am not living in a moment of enjoyment. I lack enthusiasm!

Enthusiasm is a virtue that has vanished from my life. The pressure from the negative has crushed the positive. Granted, outside influences are like throwing gasoline on a fire. For the most part, I allow this to happen. I am the one who needs to keep a smile on my face. I need to dance "The Happy Dance!"

"Dancing with the Fayetteville Stars" finally arrives and Sunday and I were both pleased with our performance. During our choreographed presentation I pull her to me, release her forward, grasp her hand, pull it swiftly over her head, and she spins around me in a clockwise direction fourteen times without hesitation. Needless to say, the audience and the other dancers are impressed. This evening I feel good about myself and the world I live in. And, I followed Terra's instructions: I smiled and did a happy dance.

Chapter Thirty-Five

Winston and Emma are two of Rufus's friends who live at the beach. Their masters walk them and we occasionally cross paths walking through the golf course at Sandpiper Bay.

"Look, Rufus, there are your buddies!" I call to him. Winston and Emma's ears perk up as they spot Rufus headed in their direction. Happy Dance! All of the dogs are doing the Happy Dance. After a few sniffs, the ground pouncing commences with Winston and Rufus. Emma watches the two from a short distance away as they play and romp.

Winston and Emma are Schnauzers. Rufus has a shaggy cut and Winston and Emma have a defined cut that highlights their silver, black, and white coats. Since the three are leashed, their motion and travel are limited. A fun time would be to let them play free in a confined area. Knowing Rufus, the fun would never end as the three scurry and scamper to and fro.

Chapter Thirty-Six

Rufus has a love for life and gives comfort. Joy can always be seen on the expressions of his glowing face. His presence gives a sense of peace and security. I am very thankful he found us and came into our lives.

Two years ago my Mother was admitted to the assisted living facility in Fayetteville. Looking back it has been a very fast-paced period of time since her needed arrival. In the beginning days, she was at the upper tier level of mental and physical demeanor. Now, she is at the lowly bottom. My Mother is dying.

I have never experienced the death of a loved one. I am not quite sure how I will handle her passing. I am normally sure of my calculated emotions. This time . . . I don't know. She was always here for me.

Dad and I arrived from the beach this afternoon. She was waiting. Although the mentally crippling disease Alzheimer's has encrusted her receptors with plaque, her spirit lives and reveals itself. Her spirit is waiting.

Three days ago I saw the love of God in her face. I honestly had not observed this over the past number of years. Instead, this born-again, spirit-filled, Christian woman appeared to have lost the joy of the Lord and was frustrated as hell due to the result of her torments from Alzheimer's. Mom was not a happy camper.

Today, Mom's eyes are open and she has a blank, motionless stare. Oxygen is introduced through her two nostrils to assist in the oxygenation of her red blood cells as they swirl through her slowing body. Though lifeless in body appearance, Mom has occasional movement in her face.

"I love you Mom," I say quietly in her left ear. Expecting her to say "I love you" or "You are mine," I silently wait for her passing. She is the best mother and never disappoints me.

Most of the family is gathered around Mom, as we await her foreseen death. Sarah and Matt are on their way from Raleigh. It is late and all are tiring. Is Mom waiting for her granddaughter Sarah's final touch and kiss goodbye? Will her spirit move forth and her earthly body cease after Sarah says farewell? Sarah and Matt have arrived at the assisted living facility and are ascending to the third floor on the elevator. Mom's respiration is fast as Sarah nears.

"Hey, Grandma . . . . hey, Grandma. She looks worse than the last time I saw her on Sunday. Her eyes look bad . . . . her eyes look bad," Sarah says, holding her brother tightly.

"Sarah, Sarah come here," I ask her to come to me. "Sarah she may be waiting for you to say goodbye . . . just talk to her spirit and say you love her."

"Hey, Grandma . . . I love you," Sarah says, softly touching Mom's face and stroking her hair. Sarah holds and prays with her grandmother. Tashia, the third-shift caregiver, comes in to check on Mom. As expected, Mom's body is relaxing and she continues to defecate frequently. The staff continues to assist in her final living.

At four in the morning, her breath ceases, and heart failure ends her earthly life. Mom's suffering and confusion are over. She was a great Mother and friend.

Mom and Dad both opted for a living will and to be cremated. The living will did not surprise me, but the cremation did. All of my known relatives are resting in graves across the country. Today my Mother's remains transitioned to a box of ashes.

The final burn has troubled me. Except for the DNA that can be possibly found on some of her personal articles, my mother no longer exists from a physical sense. Granted, there would have been no life left in her body; however, DNA would have been in the grave after her burial.

I can see visiting a cemetery but not visiting where one's ashes lie to rest, and the thought of an urn on the mantle troubles me. I know she is gone, and I believe in the after life . . . but that old Christian spiritual, "Up from the grave he arose . . ." somehow keeps circulating in my mind. I'm sure a two-hundred-year-old body is not a pretty sight, but still the DNA is there.

I often use my quote: "The only way to understand presence is when one has to deal with absence." My Mother is gone. While she lived in the assisted living facility, it was very convenient on my part to come and visit her. Even though I regularly visited and talked to her, those days are over. I will never be able to physically look into her eyes again and hear her say, "I love you . . . you're mine, you're mine."

As family and friends gather after Mom's passing, Rufus is there to greet everyone. He senses the absence of loss and is a "Little Trooper" as he helps absorb the emotional pain from family and friends.

Chapter Thirty-Seven

Dad concludes it is time for him to be admitted into the assisted living facility in Fayetteville. The struggles of keeping up the home at the beach and the often lonely nights prompt his plan to be put in action.

As people age, they have a distinguishable bell curve as it relates to their health. When Dad is at the top of the curve, he can live by himself. When he is at the bottom of the bell curve, he requires assisted living.

Also, Dad is keenly aware that a bad fall will send him into a nursing home. In a nursing home one pretty much lives in their bed, and the only physical stimulation is flipping sides. This movement helps prevent bed sores. All of us are in favor of Dad's choice, as opposed to playing Russian Roulette.

Rufus and I head to the beach to begin the job of transitioning for Dad.

IN A HOME there are thousands of items than need to be sorted. Mom had decided to keep just about every item one can imagine, and Dad had obliged. We had decided to keep the house, so I only have to deal with the belongings. Dealing with the belongings of others proves difficult.

Knowing I need to equally divide the household contents, I purchase six large moving boxes and begin deciding in which box

I will place each piece. Quickly realizing I have in front of me thousands of items, each evoking its own set of memories, I force myself to act decisively and not reminisce over each found treasure.

Rufus is troubled with the activity of the move. He senses change. I would rather let Dad continue here, and I wish Mom would have not died. But she died, and Dad can no longer live by himself, and I have to play with the dealt cards.

A WEEK later everything is in place in the house at the beach; Dad's room at the Carolina Inn is furnished, and he is ready to move into his new home.

Dad's move eases the pressure of the worries about the eventual phone call that someone has discovered him injured or unconscious. He is now in a safe environment and we are using his new home as a base. He can still return to the beach on the weekends and can attend family vacations.

Chapter Thirty-Eight

The Fayetteville Dogwood Festival is taking place this weekend. The downtown is alive and Rufus watches from the second floor balcony. So many people are walking to and fro. The new activity is both stimulating and distracting to both of us.

Instead of walking around at Festival Park, we opt to walk in the opposite direction. Rufus appears to have the gift of discernment as we walk around the downtown visitors. One moment he is this happy, cute, red-haired dog that likes everyone, The next moment, he sees a foe and the breeding of a dog guard comes forth. His growls, quick barking, and snaps keep onlookers at bay.

The thousands of adventurers have left the excitement of downtown Fayetteville and Rufus is at peace. As we walk around our usual stomping grounds, he picks up new scents and attempts to outsmart me by grasping at discarded food items . . . bringing out the dog in him . . . sometimes I forget!

Chapter Thirty-Nine

David Jr., Sarah, Matt, Louie, Rufus, and I are vacationing on Ocracoke Island, part of the Outer Banks of North Carolina. After the four-hour drive and the three-hour ferry ride, Rufus and I finally arrive. During the lengthy ferry ride Rufus is not sure of his wet surroundings. To keep him stirred up I constantly remind him, "We're getting ready to see Louie . . . you're getting ready to see Louie, Rufus!"

The East Carolina University Ferry arrives at Ocracoke and we await instructions to disembark. "OK, Rufus, the ferry mate is motioning for us to move forward . . . let's go see Louie," I tell him. Perking up, he places his front paws on the dash and assumes the bird dog position.

We drive off the ferry ramp and we immediately spot David Jr. and Sarah. As expected, Rufus jumps for joy as they quickly approach the car.

"Hey, Rufus, how's my little buddy!" David Jr. greets us, attempting to hold Rufus back.

We follow their SUV and quickly arrive at the rented beach cottage. Knowing Rufus has one thing on his mind, I release him from the security of his leash. Without hesitation he spots Louie on the deck and heads up the stairs. Happy dance, Louie and Rufus are doing the happy dance and it continues . . .

TODAY IS DAVID JR'S thirty-first birthday and we go to a local restaurant to partake in the festivities. Since Louie and Rufus are not service dogs, they remain on the deck of the beach house and wait for our return.

"Hey, Louie, when do you think the pack is going to be back?" Rufus asks, sniffing the wooden railing surrounding the deck.

"Look, Rufus . . . you're free outside and sniffing the world away . . . relax, take a few deep breaths . . . savor the moments," Louie snaps back.

"Oh, Louie, you know how I worry about Master. Sometimes I just don't know what he would do without me! And remember, if we don't wake them up in the morning, they will sleep in the burrow all day. Now, don't you agree?" Rufus asks his sparring partner.

"OK, Rufus, you're right as usual . . . just sniff, relax, and let the aromas enter your nostrils," Louie responds, as he snickers. "I caught a good smell, Rufus, the same smell from last night . . . over to your left Rufus!" Louie cries out.

". . . Yea that smells really good . . . sort of like . . . Louie, that smells better than anything I have found in Festival Park . . . this is good," Rufus says, grinning from ear to ear. Louie looks over at Rufus and thinks how sad it must be not to be able to grin from ear to ear.

"Hey, Rufus, we have a great life," Louie says, smiling. And, Rufus and Louie sniff the night away.

Chapter Forty

Bang, Bang, Bang. "Hey, Rufus, it's time to get up . . . come on, Rufus, it's time to get up . . . Rufus . . . Rufus," Louie calls out. Matt, wanting to calm Louie down, obliges and opens the door for him. With Louie out of his hair, Matt returns to bed.

Now, having to deal with both Louie and Rufus jumping around, I conclude it's a good time to take them out. As soon as Louie hits the bottom of the stairs, he makes his mark on the ground. As soon as Louie finishes, Rufus has to dominate the mark.

"That was easy!" Maybe now I can get a few more hours of sleep. "OK, guy's, let's get back upstairs," I say, somewhat pleading.

"Come on, Rufus. Let's wake up the pack. I heard them talking about going somewhere . . . ," Louie says, panting heavy.

"I want to sleep some more Louie; remember we're on vacation," Rufus replies, closing his eyes.

Continuing to walk about, Louie wakes up everyone and the day begins.

"OK, guys, let's go out on the deck . . . come on, Rufus. Come on, Louie, let's go boys," Sarah says, opening the sliding door.

"Hey, Louie are you picking up any good scents yet?" asks Rufus.

"Let's see . . . not yet. Check out the dog walking by!" Louie replies.

"Hey, Baby, how are you doing down there?" Louie calls out.

"Louie, don't talk like that," Rufus says in a scolding voice.

AFTER SPENDING THE past four nights at the beach house, Sarah, Matt, and Louie are packing up and getting ready to head back home. Having never been to Hatteras or the famous Cape Hatteras Lighthouse, Sarah and Matt change their travel venue to take the north ferry to Hatteras. David Jr. and I has also planned to visit the Cape Hatteras Lighthouse at some point during the remainder of the week. We all leave together and head north on the island.

After a short ferry ride, we disembark and head to the lighthouse. Before long we spot the lighthouse exit and turn toward the Atlantic. A fog begins to set in as we approach the parking area beside the lighthouse.

Rufus is ready to get out and see the giant post coming out of the ground. This is the best place to make a mark, he thinks to himself.

Pulling the leash hard, Rufus starts toward the lighthouse. Snap! The leash strap breaks and Rufus is off. In less than a minute, Rufus races to the base of the lighthouse, stops, sniffs, lifts his leg . . . and makes his mark.

"Hey, get away from there!" a Park Ranger yells at Rufus. Startled, Rufus gains his composure and runs out into the large field beside the lighthouse. Without warning, up he goes into the air. A few people catch the movement but with the low fog, they pay no attention. With his limbs out to the side, the wind lifts Rufus up and he is at the top of the lighthouse circling in the fog.

"This is all we need to have happen!" I exclaim. The lighthouses fall under the United States Coast Guard and the Coast Guard falls under the Department of Homeland Security, and we have a problem! I know a Park Ranger is manning the top of the lighthouse, so trouble may be brewing for Rufus. I see a glimpse of Rufus as he flies by toward the ocean shore. Rufus is flying in the low clouds, so he is pretty much invisible.

TIME PASSES AND Rufus is nowhere to be found. We search low and high . . . especially in this situation. A strong updraft would have taken him out to sea where he would have dropped into the vast ocean.

Every step I take reminds me that my little buddy is lost. Again, I am reminded that one only understands presence when dealing with absence. Rufus is gone and I may never see him again. After hours of searching, darkness is upon us, and we decide to resume the search in the morning.

DAVID JR. AND I leave for Hatteras on the first ferry in the early morning hours. Searching the perimeter of the lighthouse is once again in vain. No Rufus . . . he cannot be found. Feeling defeated, I reluctantly return to Ocracoke Island.

David Jr. and I sit silently in the car during the ferry ride to Ocracoke. We disembark and drive the long, straight road to the beach house. Before us on the ocean side of the island are a row of giant kites soaring in the air. We pull over and take some photographs of this incredible, colorful sightendless kites floating in the air.

Taking an array of photographs of the colorful shapes and animals helps take my troubled mind off Rufus. Before long, the kite navigators come over and strike up a conversation. They are both retired computer programmers and have taken up kite flying as part of their retirement.

Suddenly, in my viewfinder, I see a familiar face. It's Rufus! Rufus is flying with the other animals in the sky. With a slow, deliberate dissent, he lands beside us and once again does his happy dance.

"Rufus, I was worried to death about you. Where have you been?" I ask him.

"Well, Master, I got caught in an updraft, and I have been flying around since the last time you saw me. I saw the animals flying and I headed toward them. I knew they could help me find you . . . and here you are, Master!" Rufus tells me.

"Rufus, you are the best."

"No, Master, you are the best!" Rufus says, smiling ear to ear.

"I didn't know Rufus could talk," says David Jr.

"I bet you didn't think I could fly either," replies Rufus.

Chapter Forty-One

"Shop Cat," appears on a sunny afternoon near a roll-up door in fabrication at McCune Technology. The white and black, lanky feline has a long, thin tail, almost as long as her body.

"Rufus, come here, we have a new visitor at the building," I say, slightly pulling on his leash. Immediately, Rufus senses the movement and charges at Shop Cat. Relentlessly his new-found friend falls and lies on her back, then rubs up to Rufus.

"Hey, you were suppose to run . . . what's with you, cub?" Rufus asks.

Silence . . ." Hey, I really like your smell . . . and the way you rub up to me." Rufus says, encouraging a hopeful reply.

"Come on, Rufus, let's go into the office. I need to check my e-mail," I say, with a gentle tug on his leash. With a stronger pull, Rufus indicates he wants to stay a little longer.

OVER THE NEXT few weeks, Shop Cat fits right in. Even those who don't care for cats take to her. Food and water always appear for her and she often rest in areas where there is lots of traffic. She follows employees and customers alike and gently rubs up to them. She does it so non-confrontationally that no one knocks her away. Before long all around her realize something is different.

Tonight, David Jr. and I are working are working late near the laser and we accidentally drop a piece of steel plate on the ground. Bang! Shop Cat lies motionless. "David, did you see Shop Cat?" I ask

"I think she's deaf," he quickly replies.

I walk over and gently lift Shop Cat to my chest. As expected, she softly rubs up to me and closes her eyes. "David, drop a piece of steel on the ground," I ask. Bang! No movement.

"One more time, David," I say, moving slightly to get Shop Cat's attention. Bang!

"Yes, David, she's deaf . . . this explains a lot about her fearless personality."

FIFTEEN YEARS AGO we had a deaf employee at McCune Technology. I received a call from the local Employment Security Commission. We keep a welding position available, and they had an employee who wanted to talk with us.

Debra had been deaf since birth. She lacked the felia in the inner ears. Without this highly specialized tissue, sounds are unrecognizable. She was raised by her grandparents and they never held her back. Debra excelled in rodeo barrel racing and figure skating, competing on national levels.

In her late teens, both Debra's grandparents passed away. Even though her grandparents were well-off, Debra was not included in the will and relatives forced her out of her childhood home. Without guidance or security, she met someone and married. Years later, with three children and an abusive husband who took pride in his torment of her, Debra felt it was time to move on.

Not having a career or any secondary education, Debra became the product of welfare. Under the Workforce Development Act, she was given an opportunity to attend college while the government assisted in helping to pay her and the children's expenses.

Debra decided she would take the required courses to become a welder. She felt this was an honorable field of study. A year later, she graduated from our community college and visited the Employment Security System for job placement.

In our line of business, as it relates to metal fabrication, there are three categories of workers: those who can process steel, those who assemble, and those who weld. The desire is to have an individual who can perform well in all three functions. Debra was a welder. We had to train her to process and assemble. Her mindset was that she was only to weld. It takes years for a true craftsman to jointly be trained and train themselves.

Debra had the sole welder mindset because, "She is a welder!"

It was apparent that I needed to communicate with her and the passing of notes wasn't getting it. My thought: The analysis of the English language in her head is different than the English language in my head. I needed to build a translator. Listening to Debra talk, I observed that she pronounced the word "Car" as Khazar, and said it very slowly. With amplification and increased tempo, I could talk to her. Then she would talk, and I reduced the tempo. Sure enough, it worked. Life improved for all.

Finally, life was going good for Debra. Her story was so impressive she was awarded The Governor's Commission on Workforce Development Individual Participant of the Year. Over one thousand attendees gave her a standing ovation after she gave hand signs and a translator spoke.

Time passed and Debra met another man. She became involved, and her family and work suffered. Life began closing in on her. Finally,

Debra left without the zest of our first meeting. Once again, a needy man had taken advantage of a loving and affectionate woman.

A similar personality can be seen in Debra and Shop Cat high id, trusting and loving.

Chapter Forty-Two

Master needs to play with me. I will not be a pup forever. I noticed the other day he let the window all the way down on my side of the car. I am not a jumper out the window at any speed. Sometimes I just wonder what he thinks. Anyway, back to playing . . . I like to chase, run around, around and around; the faster I go, the happier I am. Come on just try and catch me. Nothing can stop me when I'm on a tear!

"Hey, Rufus, are you ready to go for a walk," I call out, looking for him. Within seconds here he comes, doing the happy dance and jumping more frantically than normal. "OK, Rufus, calm down so I can get your leash on . . . come on, Rufus," I firmly say, attempting to secure his collar.

Out the door Rufus runs with his head twitching back and forth and his paws in full motion. "Slow down, Rufus, we have plenty of time for our walk and I promise I will not rush you," I assure him. "In fact, Rufus, since you are in such a rush today, you lead and I'll follow," I say. And with a quick jerk, off he goes, and I follow.

IT'S FESTIVAL PARK for me today! Maybe I can finally catch one of these pesky squirrels that try my patience. They think they are so smart and cunning, but they have nothing on me. The only thing that holds me back is this leash. Some day all of you will be mine! What was that? Just a big leaf . . . one has to be careful and keep on guard, I am responsible. Dog ahead! Dog ahead! Pull hard toward the dog . . . I want to see the dog.

"Rufus, this is a new breed of dog you have never seen before. This is a Greyhound," I tell him.

"Sniff . . . sniff. Hey, you have been around a while. Look how thin you are, wouldn't hurt to fatten up a little."

"I am a retired runner, was in quite a few faces in my day Now I just lay back and take it easier."

"Wow! You must be a celebrity. Did you win many races?"

"I won my share, raced primarily down in Florida, around Tampa. Have you ever been to Florida?"

"No, but I have been to Jekyll Island, which is pretty close. Boy, it's hot there!

"In Florida it gets mighty hot, so I am very happy I am retired here where it's cooler."

"I need to resume my walk with my master. It was nice meeting you."

"Good meeting you too, Red."

He called me Red, that's odd I thought all dogs are color blind, I kind of like Red!

I wonder when we are going back to the beach.

Chapter Forty-Three

Tresia lives on the waterway in North Myrtle Beach. Boxy was her dog. She gently cared for Boxy as a pup and became the surrogate mother. Some thought both Tresia and Boxy went a little too far, as Boxy was commonly seen wearing a T-shirt. The biker's jacket pushed reactions a bit further. The drive-in employee at Wendy's will never forget the time the large Boxer wearing a t-shirt, biker's jacket, and seat belt turned her head and winked at him!

Time passed on the waterway and at an early age of three, Boxy became ill. Tresia's everything was diagnosed with cancer. After the shock, Tresia asked her vet if anything could be done: chemotherapy was a costly option and might work. In tears, Tresia and Boxy left for home.

Gaining her composure, Tresia told her family the news. All were shocked that she could even consider spending the money on chemotherapy for . . . a dog.

Tresia later contacted me and told me of her plight. Knowing her love for Boxy, I suggested Tresia proceed with the implementation of chemotherapy. Thousands of dollars later, Boxy remained in remission for four years.

The following year, Boxy had further complications and died. A special facet within Tresia left when Boxy passed. I have suggested she get another dog, and at this point she is hesitant.

"LOOK, RUFUS, THERE'S Tresia!" I call to him. Immediately, Rufus goes into fast tail wagging stance. Calming him down just a little, Tresia pulls a stuffed animal out of somewhere and, as customary, presents Rufus with a new fun toy. Dancing with joy, Rufus runs back and forth then pounces on his new cub.

As with her dressed up dog, aiding to increase the life of her dog, and showering my dog with gifts, one can say Tresia is a bit different. Let's see, 53 and the body of Barbie, the heart of Maryann, and the mind of Ginger.

For some unknown reason, Tresia was not given a middle name. Since no one could figure out how to pronounce Tresia, she gave herself a middle name, Lisa, to help in the pronunciation of Tresia, seems to work. Tresia Lisa, now that's cute.

Chapter Forty-Four

My friend Kim has posed a simple, but thought-provoking question, "David, what makes you happy?"

Without hesitation, I reply, "My family, my friends, and Rufus."

"David, you smiled," she calmly states, ". . . first time I saw you smile this evening."

A service dog helps the blind, deaf and mentally challenged with the aid of specific training. Rufus helps bring a smile to my face. I am thankful Rufus decided to venture forth and let me understand how *"A dog is man's best friend."*

A Note From The Author

In my wallet is Carl McCune's World War I USMC aluminum dog tag. Issued the 24th of October 1915, # 117887 was proudly carried by my grandfather in the European conflict. Granddaddy, a sergeant, noted photographer and writer of World War 1, even survived a mustard gas attack, gasped for life and survived the perils of war.

"Dog tag" is the informal name for the identification tags worn by military personnel, because of their resemblance to actual dog tags. The tag is primarily used for the identification of dead and wounded, along with providing religious affiliation and essential basic medical information.

Dog tags are usually fabricated from a corrosion-resistant metal or alloy. During wartime, they have been made from whatever metals were available. In the event the member has a medical condition that requires special attention, an additional red tag with the pertinent information is issued and worn along with the standard dog tags. Wearing dog tags is required at all times by soldiers in the field, and each unit designates the manner in which the tags are worn.

Today, nearly 100 years after Granddaddy's dog tag was created, RUFUS—Rapid Universal Find Us System is the dog tag of the future! Inspired by a lowly street dog wandering as a pup in downtown Fayetteville, the name Rufus is being transformed into a household word.

My love for my dog Rufus motivated me to design and create a QR Code metal dog tag. Within seconds, the Quick Response Code can be scanned by a cell phone app and POOF! one is connected to Rufus' website and all noted information is displayed via the Internet. Not only is this invention great for our four-legged friends, it has wonderful human benefits. Imagine the following scenario:

"911 can I help you?" the voice at the other end at the cell phone responds calmly.

"There's been a bad accident at mile marker 46 on I-95 south bound," the caller reports.

"Thanks for your assistance. I'll send emergency personnel to the accident scene," the 911 operator replies. Within seconds, paramedics are dispatched and on the way.

"Jim, looks like a bad collision up ahead," Stan says to his partner, as they approach the accident scene. The rescue vehicle comes to an abrupt stop and the paramedic team exits to assist the collision victims. The two men rush to the crumbled automobile and quickly assess the victims' vitals and relative condition.

"Jim, grab your phone . . . they have RUFUS!" Stan calls out.

Within seconds, the crash victims are identified and their family and personal physicians are contacted.

The RUFUS—Rapid Universal Find Us System—helps paramedics and alerts the family in the event of an unforeseen accident.

About The Author

David McCune is often referred to as a Renaissance Man. As a young child, David was always inventing or building some kind of new gadget. In his teenage years, he launched high altitude rockets with mice in the flight capsules. Later he built pollution control devices for the internal combustion engine. At nineteen, he started McCune Technology with an idea for a rear window louver for his Datsun 240-Z and a $35 dollar investment.

Now in his fifties, he is a nationally renowned artist, entrepreneur and authority on Workforce Development. His latest endeavors are acting and modeling – David finds both jobs to be challenging and a lot of fun.

He is currently finishing a book titled "Death Divorce Alzheimer's", an insightful true story and facts.

David's latest invention is the RUFUS - Rapid Universal Find Us System.